Overthinking My Way To Slay

A collection of poems on nature & love

Simran Rathore

BookLeaf Publishing

India | USA | UK

Dedication

For those who carry oceans of emotions within them but have no shore to lay their words......*this is for you.*

Preface

This book is a piece of my heart. "Overthinking my way to slay" the title symbolizes how my tendency to overthink allowed me to analyze things deeply and ultimately write these poems. I have always believed that **love** and **nature** speak the same language. Therefore, what could be a better way to express these feelings then poetry itself. This book is a collection of poems written during moments when I felt nature embracing me in times of growth and when I truly understood what it means to love someone and to be loved in return.

Writing these poems has been both a release and a revelation. I wrote them for myself, but also for you—the one who feels deeply, who finds meaning in the smallest details, who knows that love, like nature, is both wild and gentle, fleeting and eternal. This book now belongs to you, the reader. May you find the meaning, warmth, and a little bit of yourself in these pages.

Acknowledgements

I want to express my deepest gratitude to my family and friends, whose love and encouragement have been the driving force behind this collection. To my family, thank you for always believing in me and for providing a safe, loving space where my creativity could grow. Your support has meant the world to me, and without it, this book would not exist.
To my friends, thank you for your patience, your laughter, and your unwavering belief in my work. You were there through moments of doubt and triumph, and your friendship has been a constant source of strength and inspiration.
This book is as much yours as it is mine, and I am forever grateful for your presence in my life.

1. UNTANGLING THE SELF

My prudent self became
a ruffled mess,
but the feeling it brought was worth a million such tests.

Unbothered, unhinged, unbecoming,
my original self.

It was yet unknown
that I was untangling a very complex process.

Smiles, laughter, tears, and grief were part and parcel of
it all.
Imprinted memories filled my soul.

But, my oh my!
If you ask me yet again,
I would risk taking a million such tests
just to procure that feeling again!

2. BEAUTY IN COMPLEXITY

The culminating urge to say
There isn't always a way.
Sometimes, things are not meant to be untangled;
Their complexity reveals their beauty in its own way.
The heart learns to listen where words dare not stray,
And finds in the stillness, a vibrant display
In shadows where silence holds sway,
Whispers dance like leaves in a gentle ballet.
In the ebb and flow, we learn how to sway,
Catching echoes of laughter, in the light of the day.
Life consists of expressions and intrusions;
One doesn't always need to rush to match its pace.
Sometimes, unfolding it slowly is the most unique play.

3. WHO IS SHE?

She is bestowed with beauty.
She is an obscure work of art.
She is a masterpiece of precision.
People wonder what she is made of.
She burns with passion.
She is fierce.
To some, she is the world.
To others, she is an icon of admiration.
She is artistry, passionately brought to life.
Who is she?
She is a woman with a smile.
A smile that can change the world, even in the face of
plight.
She is built to endure pain and can make you a bearer of
wisdom with her insights.
She is a woman of courage, a woman beyond grief, a
woman with the power to own the world
And even you, indeed.

4. HER EYES

Her eyes snapped open,
Gazing at the wall,
Filled with tears,
Which slowly descended down her face
And finally vanished beneath her abrupt smile
A catalyst between her and the divine.
She had a turbulent look in her eyes,
One that made the world shake.
Then came the downpour.
The clouds burst,
As if nature itself was unleashing its wilderness.
Her eyes, still groaning,
Made the moment more catastrophic.
And then—suddenly—she blinked.
It was impromptu.
The weather shifted.
The clouds disappeared.
Sunshine flooded the world.
It was her eyes that spoke it all.

Eyes filled with fierceness, compassion, love, ignition,
sorrow, and grief.
Her eyes held the power of a woman
Filled with belief.

5. PARADOX

Sometimes, I feel like the eye of the cyclone
calm and collected on the outside,
but deep down,
I'm the very storm shaking the world around me.

Sometimes, I long to be alone,
to breathe in silence without interruption.
But then, just as fiercely,
I crave the kind of hug
that feels like home wrapped in arms.

The world spins wildly,
a dance of shadows and light.
while deep within, a whisper calls,
for peace to replace the fight.

Sometimes, I crave attention.
And sometimes, in a room full of people,
I feel completely abandoned.
but each smile feels like a jagged dart.

Sometimes, I wear a mask so bright,
hiding storms that brew just out of sight.
I sway with laughter, play the part.
Sometimes, I find solace in the night,
where the stars blanket my worries in gentle light.
The contrast of chaos, the stillness of the moon,
they hold me softly and hum a quieter tune.

6. VALIDATION GARDEN

My self-criticizing, self-deprecating self
Came to a halt
a pause I hadn't felt.
I finally saw it wasn't all my fault;
Growth takes time, and wounds aren't asphalt.

Everything evolves, nothing stays the same,
And I get to choose who plays in my mental game.
I spent so long chasing validation in disguise,
Living for a nod, a like, a look in someone's eyes.

That approval gave me a dopamine high,
Like standing in a garden where the trees scrape the sky.
But even lush trees face their drying season
And that's when I learned: there's always a reason.

People leave when their part in your story ends,
Not every chapter is meant to hold the same trends.
The ones who stay won't need constant light
They'll hold on even through your silent nights.

7. CHAOTIC MESS

"Poets are chaotic," they said.
But how else would they create
a mess that makes sense?
A storm that speaks?

"Poets are insane," they claimed.
But that madness
it comes from souls set free,
from minds unchained,
too vast for the everyday eye to see.

When a spirit lives beyond the rules,
its rhythm doesn't match the clocks.
It dances at odd hours,
writes truth in metaphors,
and bleeds meaning onto the page.

You call it chaos
we call it art.

And in the silence after the poem ends,
in the ache between the lines,
there lies a truth too sharp to say aloud
that maybe the world was never meant
to understand us,
only to feel us
and be forever changed.

8. ROLLERCOASTER

Life is a rollercoaster, wild and steep,
Spinning through turmoil, robbing sleep.
But what if we let our desires unwind,
Chased them freely, left fear behind?

Let's wander the world, laugh in the rain,
Unlearn our worries, relearn play.
Can we become children once more
Hearts wide open, spirits sore?

Dreams like kites in a summer sky,
Soaring bold, refusing why.
Reach for stars with trembling grace,
Find new hope in empty space.

Hold my hand when the teardrops fall,
My joy comes in seasons—rare, and small.
Let's paint the dawn in hues brand new,
Where every heartbeat whispers, "I believe in you."

Wrap the moments in shimmering light,
Turn our sorrows into wings in flight.
From aching truths, let beauty bloom
Even the night makes space for the moon.

9. NOT FOR ME

Saw ocean-deep eyes, filled with emotions
but the emotions were never for me.
I saw tears and fears trace their face;
has anyone ever analyzed them
as deeply as I did?

Why did I feel every flicker of their soul,
every silent scream,
when none of it was meant for me?

That's when I realized
they are an indelible part of my life,
but to them,
I was never even a chapter.

I craved their attention,
their love,
even their fear
but it was never mine to hold.
I wanted them to know the storm within me

how fiercely I ached for the love they gave.
Not to me,
but to someone else.
I longed to be theirs,
to be held in the warmth I watched from afar,
to drown willingly
in a sea I was never meant to touch.

This time, I won't long.
I'll take a step back
and let them see
that I carry oceans in my eyes
and they are definitely
not for me.

10. WHEN SILENCE SPOKE

She never found the words.
So she stayed quiet
a silence stitched
with secrets no one could unspool.

They tried to read her stillness,
to decode the hush
behind her eyes.
But years passed,
and her truth remained tucked
beneath a single fear,
and the slow fall of a frown.
She answered only with silence.

Until the day
her quiet cracked.

She spoke
and the world bent to listen.
Every hidden wound,

every buried wrong,
rose like smoke in the wind.

The sky dimmed.
The world, awestruck,..
And in all this clash,
all that remained
was the never ending love of a mother towards her
children,
she derailed her calm,
survived the wildfires,
only for her children to live the way they Desire.

11. CAREFREE SOUL

A carefree soul
not that attached, not too sore,
so chill, so obscure.
And then came the day:
this soul was not carefree anymore.

It felt.
It delved into emotional flight.
It kept on chasing one direction
the only one that felt right.

The soul was intertwined with another;
the other made the heart stutter, flutter.
The heart that never settled for one
now refused to seek someone new.

It only wanted that same soul
to stay, to see it through.

But this time, that soul drifted,

free of the weight that anchored it.
Maybe they weren't meant to stay,
only to show the other
what it means to feel.

12. WINDOWPANE

What does those wild eyes contain?
a rollercoaster of emotions still acting sane
finding beauty in little things so there is nothing to
complain
just like a raindrop on my windowpane.
they whisper secrets of joy and pain
each heartbeat dances, caught in the frame,
a symphony of laughter, with sorrow's refrain,
moments collide, in a delicate chain.

13. SEA SHORE

Standing on the seashore, all alone,
Hearing the waves roar,
Made my heart pound.

Was it just me,
Or the howling wind's sound?

My feet in the sea
Synchronized me with a world so new.
A world with no lies,
Only stars glowing in the night sky.

The clutter in my head dispersed.
The mesmerizing effect of the sea
Was interspersed.

Within moments, the night was gone.
Red light scattered,
And it was dawn.

14. OCEAN

Is it never-ending...
What would standing amidst it be like...
I wondered.
The currents, the waves, the tides,
rising up and down constantly,
made my heart feel relieved.
The melodious voice it made
made me even more intrigued.
The reflection caused by it
made the whole night bright.
I gazed into it with a smile
and saw the little child I was,
now grown up,
but still with the same exuberance.
It was the ocean I was looking at.
The ocean I love.
The place with peace...

15. NATURE

Can you feel the nature?
The thought of the Earth's curvature
sliding left to right
in the middle of the night...

The magnificent roars
of the sea shores,
miscellaneous chores,
lava filled in the bores.

The circle of illumination,
filled with uncertain hallucinations.
The shine and brilliance
of stars as far as a gazillion.

Does it strike you as well?
Does it make your heart excel?
It makes me want to yell
that this is the nature in which I want to dwell.

16. ECHOES OF THE UNIVERSE

What does the universe, in turn, bring to you in
response?
The woven threads representing the bonds,
the lies tied in a scuffled head,
the magical goodbyes of the sun ahead.

Raindrops turning into hail,
fire frowning in the forest—yet still, it prevails.
The charismatic breeze is seized,
as if nature is locked in with shadows
and has lost the keys.

What we give is what we get
a mirror held without regret.
If we take too much and never give,
how long will the universe let us live?

17. DESTINY

The way the stars don't twinkle,
but are destined to twinkle to us.
The way the moon doesn't shine,
but still lightens the night.
The way, when the east shines,
the west sleeps in the dark.
Just like that, one cannot win the game
without the thorns being part of the path.

Destiny plays its role.

a silent hand that writes in air,
we chase, we run, we rise, we fall,
but it already knows we're there.
It bends the light, it shifts the road,
it plants the seed before the show.
Not loud, not kind, not always fair,
but always present, always aware.

Destiny plays its role.

18. LIFE HAPPENED

Life happened
when a single text from you made my heart smile.
Life happened
when you became my 11:11 wish.
Life happened
with flickers of your face in my mind.
Life happened
the day song lyrics finally started to make sense.
Life happened
when you became the only thing I couldn't stop talking
about.
Life happened
when the only notification I waited for—was yours.
But life truly happened
when you became a certain someone,
and I realized,
you were just a minuscule part of my world.
All this time,
life was already happening.
You just gave it a little sparkling light.

19. DETACHMENT

Anxious attachment—an issue, they said,
It overpowers the normal emotions we tread.
A vicious cycle, often untold,
That only a few have the strength to uphold.

Grasping for comfort, yet feeling controlled,
Fragile connections like glass, easily rolled.
It takes real strength to be brave and bold,
To reshape your beliefs, let your story unfold.

To break free from the chains that confine,
To heal the wounds—both yours and mine.
The heart seeks solace, a truth to behold,
While fear whispers softly, hiding the gold.

Yet in the tempest, a light may appear
A flicker of hope, dissolving the fear.
With patience and courage, the past can unwind;
In the warmth of connection, true love you'll find.

20. ESSENCE

Beauty lies in the very essence of every creation.
The cumulonimbus clouds, the elevated land
Forming gentle mounds by nature's hand.
The magnificent wild, with quiet elation,
Healing countless hearts, a soothing salvation.

The rustling leaves sing songs of grace,
The stars spill gold across time and space,
Even the winds, in their restless race,
Whisper truths no mirror can replace.
For every crack and every scar,
Nature crowns them as they are.

21. LOVE THAT ALIGNS

A love that aligns,
With intentions unclouded, not dipped in disguise.
To take a stand, it needs a spine.
Is it so rare to find love in our time?
A love so pure,
Where a single glance could promise a cure.
Time slips by, and love letters pile by the door,
While no one recalls what the men in war bore.

As screens glow bright and silence grows loud,
We crave connection, lost in the crowd.
Let courage rise and tenderness unfold,
For the stories of lovers are endlessly told.
Is it too much to ask for more?
Who decides what we're meant to adore?
Love isn't begged for, or distant and cold.
It's warmth,
A feeling that clings,
A steady hand that never lets go.